A
SUCCESSFUL
and PROVEN GUIDE
for the FIRST TIME
HOMEBUYER

Putting It All Together

JUDITH DICKSON

PAGE PUBLISHING, INC.
New York, NY

First originally published by Page Publishing, Inc. 2016

ISBN 978-1-68348-199-7 (pbk)
ISBN 978-1-68348-200-0 (digital)

Printed in the United States of America

Acknowledgments

When writing a book, it is important to work alongside competent people, who can offer you their advice. I was very fortunate to have had this opportunity with a group of exceptional people who had years of experience behind them.

I am acknowledging these professional people and I express my heartfelt thanks to all of you. They are Mrs. Salamone Kirkutis who is the manager and owner of SKS Realty with over twenty years of experience. We chose her because of the extent of knowledge she has as a real estate agent and the time she took to assist us with our home purchase. Mr. Brian McGuirk, who is also an agent within her office and Mr. Michael Kirkutis, a broker, and educated me regarding various types of loans which I will detail later in this book.

I want to recognize an author who I consider my mentor is Gail Sheehy, a *New York Times* best seller, *Daring: My Passages: A Memoir.* She is an amazing writer who never lets anything get in her way, she keeps moving forward as a writer who has experiences life's tough moments, she still keeps moving forward, a real trail blazer.

I acknowledge Mr. Richard A, Breed, Village Mortgage, West Hartford, CT., Senior Loan Originator who worked with Robert and me to obtain a first mortgage.

Contents

Introduction

> So buy now you have likely already weighed the benefits and decided that that home ownership is the best direction for you. That is a major hurdle now passed. You are focused and are ready to begin, good.
>
> —*Homebuying.com*

Now that you feel confident to search for homes, perhaps the best way to begin is to surf the internet for possibilities. Some search engines to research are Homebuying.com, Realtor.com, Trullia.com, Bankrate.com. These are just a few of the excellent resources available as well as real estate companies, virtual tours or homes, including condominiums, attached homes, townhouses, duplexes and private homes.

At this point in time you may have an idea of what type of home would best suited for you or you may still need time to research other possibilities. One idea to take into account is whether the neighborhood is within an acceptable range to your workplace. Is the setting one which you would choose to reside in: urban, rural, or suburban.

Does the community have recreational parks; if you have children, are there acceptable school systems, shopping areas, including: restaurants healthcare facilities as hospitals within an appropriate range, an emergency walk-in clinic and is your physician, dentist within reasonable proximity of your home.

Let us first begin with a "Realty Check." This is the time we have to assess what type of home we want vs. what we can afford. Suggestion: Do not ask friends or relatives their opinions, this will be your home and you should make this important decision with you and your real estate agent, when you are ready.

Remember before taking your first step, ask yourself, why do you want to buy a home? This is one of the most important and emotional decisions you will make in your lifetime. Try not to make a decision with your emotions; rather be rational and honest with yourself.

You need stability and a desire to commit for at least five to seven years. Understanding your priorities will make it that much easier to make your real estate decisions. Homeownership is a great way to increase your personal wealth for you your family, since it builds equity over time as the mortgage is paid. One other word of advice, estimate the difference between your current rent and buying a home. In a lot of instances, purchasing a home is less expensive than renting. But if for some reason you are not ready, rent until the time is right for you.

To make this decision easier for "You the Buyer," create a financial worksheet, include the following:

What financial situation you are in now, including: Financial obligations you have now, what money (cash reserves), you have set aside for your purchase, "do not let the well run dry," have a good sum of money for other living expenses. There is a life after a home purchase.

Real estate fees, mortgage fees, inspector fees and attorney fees
Closing costs
Insurance policy premium
Be prepared for any fluctuations in taxes
Repair or replacement of any appliances

In addition, check all of your credit scores, mortgage lenders will take this into account when formulating your interest rate. The higher your score, the less interest rate you will incur.

There are four major credit reporting agencies that you should contact to verify your information, and dispute anything negative that may have been reported as soon as possible:

They are:

Equifax—Customer Correspondence—PO Box 740193,
     Atlanta, GA 3037
Trans Union—PO Box 8070. North Olmstead,
     OH 44070-8070
Experian—4754 Anton Blvd., Costa Mesa, TX 92626
TRW—12606 Greenville Avenue, PO Box 749,
     Dallas, TX 75374

Credit.com—free credit report including breakdown of credit scores into sections and will give you a grade for each.

Please be aware that banks expect you to have 25–38 percent of your gross monthly income before taxes made available to them at the time you meet with them. So bring your most recent income tax return. Others lenders have stricter guidelines, so the lower your debt-to-income ratio, the better your chances of a loan approval.

Your credit score is based upon:

Your history of bill paying on time
How high your outstanding debts are
What length of time you have had credit
How high is your balance compared to your credit line; if this
     figure is too high above your balance, that will appear as
     a negative
What number of credit cards do you have/or applied for in a year

All of these aspects will be taken into account before for a pre-approval letter will be issued by your lender. This letter is sent to the mortgage department of the bank and reviewed before the final mortgage approval is issued. This allows you to have a pride of ownership that you will attain from owning your home along with the freedom of decorating without permission of the landlord. Home buying is an investment and a hedge against inflation, it is also an excellent tax shelter, provides property tax deductions, and as long as you have lived in your home from two to five years, you can exclude $250,000 for an individual and $500,000 for a married couple of profit from capital gains in your tax return.

Homeowners Tips:

If you own a condominium, you own the interior of your unit (walls within your living space). Condominium dues must be included in your monthly budget as well as your mortgage. Your condominium dues will cover outdoor maintenance, i.e., lawns, maintaining the grounds, including the swimming pool and patio. The monthly mortgage covers the interior, just like rent.

Home-ownership is a reward for wisely managing your life and money, and building your financial security and equity. It also takes thirty years to pay off your mortgage, unless you prefer to pay it off earlier.

The government subsidizes homebuyers' mortgage interest payments with a tax deduction for the first $500,000 of profit when they sell.

Integrity, Honesty
Business sophistication
Have at least ten years in the business
Knowledge of towns that you are interested

***Are sensitive to your needs and are not in a rush to sell

Questions to ask the agents:

Ask what their average list-price-to-sales-price ratio is.
Ask whether you can review documents beforehand that will have to be signed; agency disclosures, listing agreement, and seller disclosure.

Ask how much they charge.

Ask whether they offer a guarantee offer; if you are unhappy with the arrangement, will the agent let you cancel the agreement.

What is your best marketing plan or strategy for my needs?

How will you search for my home?

Hiring a Real Estate Agent

The best suggestions I can make when locating a real estate agent is:

Do not look through the yellow pages
Do not attend open houses
Do not ask family or friends

Do look for a real estate agent who has their own office and they should have the following traits:

Integrity, honesty
Business sophistication
Have at least ten years in the business
Knowledge of towns that you are interested

***Are sensitive to your needs and are not in a rush to sell

Questions to ask the agents:

Ask what their average list-price-to-sales-price ratio is
Ask whether you can review documents beforehand, which will need to be signed; agency disclosures, listing agreement, and seller disclosure and how much do they charge
Ask whether they offer a guarantee offer; if you are unhappy with the arrangement, will the agent let you cancel the agreement
What is agents' best marketing plan and strategy
How many homes will I likely see before I find a home I like?
Will I be competing against other buyers?

How do you handle multiple offers?

Do you present multiple offers yourself?

Will you please provide references?

Ask if you may call the references with questions.

The agents' rights to you are to:

Negotiate a contract with you, attend inspections and
    appraisals, offer mortgage companies

Be present at the closing

**Make your expectations known

Be selective, make sure your agent is working for *you* and I repeat, make sure they are not in a rush to sell. Trust your instincts and never forget this is your hard-earned money and your home is one of the largest investments you will make in your lifetime. Make sure you have a good comfort level with your agent and trust them.

To digress, I would like to tell you a short story about our first home-buying experience to give you an idea of our experience

We had rented for several years in apartment buildings and then relocated to a high-rise building which were a combination of apartments and condominiums. We were not planning to purchase here; however, one day I noticed a photograph on the bulletin board of a one bedroom condominium located on the second floor facing the pool. The price was right for us, so we made an appointment with the real estate office.

We took a look at it and was so amazed how well kept it was by the former owner, the walls were painted in colors that were compatible with our furnishings, there was an open kitchen with granite countertops and plenty of shelving and the appliances were in very good condition.

There were no cracks in the walls, the hardwood floors were in excellent condition and we had feeling of openness. It did not take long for us to proceed with the process applying for the condominium. We were fortunate to have the real estate company within the building. My significant other used his bank to apply for a mortgage. We finally moved in and never regretted it.

There are several internet web sites you can research for a real estate agent and also they will offer photographs of homes for sale and the name of the company handling them. Here are a list of them:

Zillow.com
MLS—Multiple listings of services

The major real estate companies are:

ERA
Coldwell Banker
Remax
Berkshire Hathaway
Prudential

An excellent resource to read is *Nolo's Encyclopedia of Everyday Law*. This book offers you the legal aspects of buying your home. It is easy reading offers an array of information, including:

Buying a house, selling your house, and deeds
Neighbors, boundaries, fences, trees, views, and noise

This book can also be found at your local library.

Remember your agent is not working for the seller. The agent is paid by the seller from the proceeds of the sale. Work with one real estate agent without the listing agent, this will lower the commission, and save you money.

One last word of advice, make sure that the purchase offer should be contingent on:

- Obtaining financing at an interest rate, but does not exceed a certain percentage that you can afford.
- The home inspection should not reveal any major problems.
- The seller must disclose any known problems within their home.
- The pest inspection does not reveal any infestations within the home.
- The seller will complete any known repairs.

Accessing Your Financial Situation and Insurance Coverage

As we discussed in the excerpt section of this book, it is really important to make sure that you have your finances in order to make a
home purchase. To reiterate, be reasonable what you can and can-
not afford. You should have very little debt, including credit cards,
school loans or any other financial obligations. You will need money
set aside for real estate fees, mortgage fees and closing fees with an
attorney. If you feel as though you may want to test the waters before
buying, you always have the option to rent a condominium to see if
the general climate is what you are seeking. It is a good way to meet
your neighbors, board of directors, get to know the environment,
and the surrounding neighborhood. If you like living there, there
are always opportunities to purchase condominiums. There are also
additional amenities as a swimming pool and a gym, and a twenty-
four-hour security with enclosed mail boxes.

If you believe you do have the funds to purchase and will still
have enough funds to live, make payments on your vehicle, (unless
of course, you own the vehicle outright); pay insurance premiums,
homeowners, healthcare, car insurance, groceries, medical expenses,
and have a stellar credit rating, plus have a cushion for the unex-
pected, then by all means buy.

Homeowners' insurance is a prerequisite to apply for a home. This insures your home including structures, personal property. If you have jewelry, fine arts, and antiques, you should purchase a rider.

In case you may live in a federal flood zone. Federal authorities can declare your area is eligible for disaster relief in order to rebuild your home and make it whole again.

If anyone is injured on your premises, it provides medical expenses. If your home is damaged is and uninhabitable, your policy will cover temporary housing as well as meal allowances, until you can re-enter your home.

Let me explain some other aspects of your homeowners policy, the higher your deductible, the less expensive your insurance will be. The following are also covered under your policy:

Dwelling and personal property are covered.
Lightning, wind, hail, theft, riot, civil commotion, fallen objects, vandalism, malicious mischief/freezing of plumbing system
Weight of ice or snow
Explosion
Sudden and accidental bulging or water discharge of plumbing or appliances as heating and cooling systems
Replacement value of your home—this only pays a preset amount, be sure your coverage is enough to cover your actual rebuilding costs.

Another aspect to consider is protection class for homeowners. This will indicate how vulnerable a home is to fire. Your home would be best to be close to a fire hydrant and a fire department. Emergency dispatch systems, the communities' telephone network, and the emergency number in the phone book. One drawback is your deductible may be too high in some cases, insurance companies may not cover this protection.

Location, Location, Location

"Location, location, location" has been in use since 1926 according to the *New York Times*. The critical reason location matters in purchasing your home is that you want to live in a safe neighborhood, where there is little crime or none at all.

There are some gated and developed communities that are popular. They have 24/7 security services, and advanced fire alarms. You should feel comfortable to walk around outside and interact with your neighbor. Each neighborhood has a certain personality. For example, do you choose to live in an inner city, surrounded by families, college students, or do you want a quiet remote area.

Living within a good school district is also an important consideration. Whether or not you have children, the better the school district, the higher the value of the homes will be. There should be commercial districts nearby which offer shops, restaurants, and public libraries. If you can purchase a home near the water this will certainly increase the value of your home. Be in close proximity to public transit to a bus and train station. Having a shorter commute to work is always another perk. In addition, make sure there is a fire, police department, and a hospital nearby, but not so close that you will be bothered by alarms and sirens.

The best way to research different locations is to travel around several communities and bring a camera to take photographs of the neighborhoods, and make a list of what matters to you most and discuss these with you real estate agent. Also try and speak to any of the people living in the area, this can make a difference in your decision process.

Check zoning laws for your property and surrounding areas, your agent can be very helpful with this. Zoning laws determine the types of businesses allowed in commercial area and the proximity to commercial to residential.

Hiring an Appraiser

This next step of hiring an appraiser should take place when *you are ready to purchase the property* you are interested in.

An appraisal is necessary is a necessary step for a *qualified appraiser* because they will understand the elements that combine to make a home worth more or less than the asking price.

Levels of Licensing:

Ask if they are licensed, (state or certified) and if they are a member of a national association, they can also be a master or a senior appraiser. You should ask for their resume, this is more of an official document that would list their credentials, training, areas of specialization, how long they have been in business and what associations they belong to.

Watch the Appraiser:

Ask questions during this process, and make sure you receive a copy of the appraisal if you hired the appraiser unless the bank hired the appraiser; then, they would receive this copy, ask them for a copy as well, it is the law. Review it carefully.

Comps:

A professional appraiser will give you the comps and the specific condition of your home compared to other homes. This refers to its age, size, roof, foundation, and whether there is lead paint. (Comps pertain to houses that had sold within the past twelve months.) The appraiser should come up in with a higher value than a tax assessor will.

Most appraisals should come within a $5000 of a comparable home; in case there is a $25,000 difference, something is wrong, hire another appraiser. The average cost to hire an appraiser is between $300 to $400 and should take approximately two hours.

The reasons you should have an appraisal of your home:

The bank needs an accurate estimate of a homes' value when it lends you the money to purchase. If a bank lends more than the worth of a house, would mean that the bank does not have enough collateral to guarantee you the loan. Because some appraisers' work with a bank regularly, they may tell the bank that a property needs to appraised for in order for a loan to go through. If these appraisers' want repeated business, they would follow the bank to ensure the loan is approved. There is a possibility of "collusion" between banks and appraisers' make sure your questions are answered and all is "above-board."

According to the *New York Times*, more than 60 percent of appraisals are overvalued.

There are two associations that may be useful to contact in hiring an appraiser:

The American Society of Appraisers (private association)
555 Hendron Parkway, Suite 125
Harden, VA 20190
(704) 478-2228

Appraiser Foundation (private, nonprofit)
1029 Vermont Avenue NW Suite 900
Washington, DC 2005-3517
(202) 347-7772

Hiring a Licensed HVAC Inspector

Looks can be deceiving, but within the inspection stage of your home it still holds true. Everything that *you* see may look perfect, but you need another set of eyes that is a professional and can see any potential problems within the structure of your prospective home. You can ask your real estate agent for a referral, if they have had many years of selling and if they are experienced enough, they can refer an inspector who should be the same caliber of your agent. So if you feel your agent is honest, ethical, and has the experience, let them suggest a qualified HVAC inspector. You can also verify with the Better Business Bureau to check for any positive or negative reviews from other clients.

The HVAC inspector should disclose any issue with the furnace, air conditioning units, appliances, electrical outlets, and make sure the voltage is not too high. Some homes and condominiums they should examine the interior of the chiller and make sure that the motor is running at an adequate capacity, filters are clean, plus the interior of the chiller baseboard which is usually made of fiberglass is clean; if it is discolored or black, this should be replaced for health reasons, there can be respiratory problems in the long run, the expense of replacing any of the elements is worth it. Your agent can also negotiate repairs or advise the buyer to walk away if the home inspection presents too many problems.

Do not forget to ask questions to the inspector over the phone before any commitment is made:

> Are you familiar with this type of home?
> Do you specialize in residential or commercial property?
> Are you a member of any professional organizations, i.e., American Society of Home Inspectors?
> How long have you been in business?
> Can I be present during the home inspection? If they say no, move on.
> Do you carry "errors and omissions" insurance. If they say no, ask why. Why not?
> Do you offer a guarantee? This may be valuable to you, if something goes wrong within this guarantee period, some firms will offer the buyer a written agreement that they are obligated to reimburse you within the time constraints of the guarantee agreement.

Be aware if the agent hires an inspector and if nothing goes wrong, the agent receives a commission and the inspector gets a repeat business. This is referred to as conflict of interest. The purchase of your home may be the largest investment in your lifetime. So the time you take to have your home completely inspected will be worth its weight in gold. There is also advice that states: In addition to getting a whole house inspected, get a heating and cooling (HVAC) inspection done by a qualified heating and cooling contractor. Why you may ask? Due to the fact that 50 percent of claims are paid on HVAC systems, yet there are two under inspected items in the whole house inspection such as the evaluation of other systems.

For example: a homebuyer may get a review from a home inspector their furnace appears functional; however, that furnace may have a crack in it and may need cleaning. There are additional tests that a HVAC contractor may do, as carbon monoxide testing, and a pressure test or using scope to check for a cracked heat exchanger, this is a frequent cause of a furnace denial claim due to pre-existing conditions. If this is not checked, repairs and replacements are costly and can cost thousands of dollars.

Here is a home inspection checklist that you may find worthwhile:

- Have the inspector check the foundation of the basement for any signs of termites or wood decay, make sure there is enough space for water leakage after wet weather.
- Check walkways and driveways for cracks, and soil erosions.
- Check doors and windows for rotted wood, window trim, broken glass, check for loose putty, any hardware should be lubricated, weather stripping should be tight, caulking of doors, windows and all openings, including joints between brick.
- Exterior walls—masonry should not have cracks, if peeling of paint, the buyer should contact the Department of Health for Lead Paint Inspectors.
- Roofs—Look for damaged or loose shingles.
- Vents should be open.
- Masonry chimneys should not have cracks (interior/exterior).

It may also be to your advantage to hire a licensed electrician to check for electrical issues which will be explained later on in this chapter. If you should have any further questions on hiring a HVAC inspector, call or write:

The American Society of Home Inspectors (ASHI)
85 Algonquin Road
Arlington Heights, III. 6005-4423

In considerations of indoor air quality and insulation call or write:

Consumer Product Safety
Washington, DC 20207
Phone: 1-800-638-2772

At the buyers' request, the lender can have a termites' inspector for less than $100 scheduled in your home to make sure there are no serious damages. To be honest, we should have been more knowledgeable about home inspectors and guarantees. A few months after we purchased, our stove had to be replaced. There was an electrical outlet in one of our cabinets in the kitchen, and we found out that the voltage was two hundred, we had to hire an electrical who stated that if you had touched this with wet hands you would have had a bad electrical shock. He took out the wiring and covered the plate of the outlet.

Also we have air chillers and not a standard air-conditioner, we felt as if the chillers were not as cold as they should have been in the summer, so we had to replace two motors and we now make sure that the vents are clean. It is important information to be sure your HVAC inspector is licensed, and you should be present at the time he is in your home. Make a list of any questions and do not hesitate to ask. Some practical information to be aware of after your home inspection:

Your home may still have problems after the inspection:

After your inspection your home may still need repairs and your inspector should communicate these to you. Mold, radon, and asbestos may be present in your home. Asbestos must be looked at carefully.

For instance, when we purchased our condominium, we were told that asbestos exists inside the walls on the bottom of the closets; however, if you do not upset these areas, there will not be a problem, you can still hang artwork or whatever on your walls, put shoes on in your closet.

If you decide to purchase a private home make sure the base-ment is not wet; if it is, this may present a problem and needs to be addressed.

Your inspector can do so much, but he should be forthright and honest with his findings and projections. Just be cognizant that he should be honest and forthright about any impending repair.

If any inspections by the inspector or electrician reveal any problems, you have the right to negotiate the homes' purchase price to reflect the cost of any damages/repairs you will need to make.

As far as hiring a licensed electrician as I mentioned previously, the following is a checklist of questions that you, the buyer, should ask an electrician:

- What is the electrical capacity of safety limits?
- Lighting and switch safety—are they grounded and attached properly and secure.
- Electrical devices—make sure the wring is updated with no electrical shortages.
- Circuit breaker and fuse safety—if a fuse blows, these should be replaced with GFCI (Ground Fault Circuit Interrupters) can be used on circuits exposed to areas near water.

In addition, they also can be used in bathrooms and kitchens

- Light bulb safety—compact fluorescent bulbs only use a fourth of the energy that incandescent bulbs do.
- Cord and plug safety—have checked for cuts and defects

Hiring a Mortgage Banker

The best suggestion I want to give you is to research your banks mortgage department and see what their rates are, this depends on what type of mortgage you want. Check your credit report and make sure it is up to date.

Please remember the first thing a mortgage broker or lender will want is your credit report, make sure there are no errors or discrepancies, if there are correct them as soon as possible. This will delay the process and present you as a higher risk and will result in a higher interest rate.

Understand your debt-to-income ratios and how much *you* can afford. If your own payment is less than 20 percent, you will have to pay "private mortgage insurance." This will be included in your monthly payment for your mortgage. The larger the down payment, the less money you will need to borrow, this results in a lower monthly payment.

Do not forget recurring debt as: car payments, credit card payments child support, student loans and other financial obligations when determining the monthly payment you can afford. The best rule of thumb is to get prequalified once you know how much you can afford. This is an informal agreement between you and the lender. There is no credit check, no charge, and you are not obligated to use this lender as your mortgage provider. This will give you a better negotiation position with the seller.

When shopping around for a lender, visit your bank and speak with their loan officer to see what types of loans are currently available at what rates. The difference between a lender and a broker is:

a mortgage lender will lend you the money directly and will decide whether to approve your mortgage and extend credit. They can also act as brokers, so ask.

A broker is an intermediary who deals with a number of different lenders to obtain your loan. They can also work with "wholesale" lenders. These lenders will only accept applications from a mortgage broker, not from the borrower. A broker is not your agent you should compare rates and loan products. Understand and choose the type of mortgage that will fit your needs.

Make sure you understand the type of mortgage you are seeking, whether it be fixed or adjustable.

****To be considered: any increase in taxes or homeowners insurance will have an effect on your monthly payment, if they increase those items will be escrowed and as part of your mortgage payment.

The Federal Reserve Board has a "mortgage comparison calculator," which allows you to compare your monthly payments and the amount of equity you will build in your home for fixed and adjustable-rate mortgages. Pay attention to the Good Faith Estimate (GFE) and Truth-in-Lending (TIL) disclosures.

Within three business days after receiving your application, the lender must provide you with or mail you a card, a GFE and a TIL. *Look closely* at these documents to make sure that the mortgage you have applied for is what the lender is actually processing. Question any charges that appear out of the ordinary; if there are questions, notify your broker or lender. This is not a contract to lend. It is an estimate of costs you will be required to pay at the closing.

Rate Locks: Connecticut law states that any rate lock be in writing. If you do not have a written rate lock this means that your rate is "floating" and can fluctuate until you close on the loan.

Get this in writing. Do not accept a verbal agreement, you will have little recourse if this is not is not in writing. Rates can change between the time that your application was submitted and closing.

Underwriting: When you have a loan product this will be underwritten. The lender will verify your credit history, financial history, have an appraisal of the property and then decide whether or not to approve your loan. At times, you may be offered a counteroffer if your credit has had problems, be wary, this can mean a change of loan terms or can change the loan terms substantially.

If the terms of a counteroffer does not make sense to you, refuse this, ask for a denial of the original loan, so that you may be reimbursed for any deposit you gave to the seller of the property.

Loan Types:

Conventional: This is a loan that is secured by real estate and made at the risk of the lender, without benefit of any government guarantee or government insurance. They may be insured by private mortgage insurance companies, which reduces the lenders' risk.

Conforming: The Federal National Mortgage Association (FNMA); better known as Fannie May, to purchase and securitize mortgages to ensure funds are available to lending institutions for home buyers. The Federal Home Loan Mortgage Corporation (FHLMC). Better known as Freddie Mac, a government entity, is to expand secondary markets for mortgages, which buy mortgages on the secondary market, pools them, and then sells them as mortgaged-backed securities to investors.

Nonconforming: These are mortgage loans in which the loan amount exceeds the Fannie Mae and Freddie Mac loan limits. These types of loans are typically not sold to either of the above entities.

FHA: This is the Federal Housing Administration, which is a division of the US Department of Housing and Urban Development (HUD). These divisions are to insure FHA mortgage loans, expand homeownership opportunities, increase minority homeownership, make the home buying process less complicated and expensive and to assist the homeowners in avoiding foreclosure.

The Attorney
and Your Closing

After your mortgage has been approved, a loan closing is scheduled. This is the final step for home ownership. You should have your own attorney represent you or if you do not have one, ask your realtor if they can suggest one for you or research yourself by using Martindale Hubbell, this an excellent resource and is found in public libraries. This will offer you hundreds of attorneys with different areas of law, you want a real estate attorney. You can interview them over the telephone or e-mail them if they offer this information. Make sure they are accessible to speak with, so you will not always have to deal with a lot of voicemails.

Be aware that your own attorney will be looking out for your best interests. Your chosen attorney will explain each document to you and they should reflect the terms of the mortgage that you had applied for. Be sure you understand the note and the settlement statement as well as the final Truth-in-Lending (TIL) disclosure. Your attorney should receive copies of these documents within twenty four hours prior to the closing. This time will allow you the time to review the statements and make sure there are no issues or if need be, reschedule the closing if you do not agree with the terms. There is a slight possibility that copies may not be provided within twenty-four hours of the closing, so make sure you read them at the time of the closing and ask any questions. The note is a legally binding document which specifies your financial responsibilities to the lender. It will include: Your loan amount, interest rate, payment amount (principal), maturity date, if there should be an increase in interest, (if the loan is adjustable to rate transaction, prepayment penalties, late charge and default information. should be disclosed).

The settlement statement will show the disbursement of the loan including: costs which you will required to pay, try to negotiate the closing costs because some costs may be inflated and you should be aware of this.

Compare these costs to the original costs disclosed on the Good Faith Estimate (GFE). These costs should be close to the to your actual cost of closing. Check these costs carefully and if you should find substantial differences, cancel the closing.

The final TIL will disclose the total cost of the transaction. The APR, finance charge, and payment schedule should be close to the TIL you received at the start of the process.

A title search and title insurance should be handled by your attorney. This will provide a legal safeguard so that no one else can claim it.

In addition, there is "open escrow" since there are many facets to complete a home sale, have a neutral third party hold all monies and documents related to the transaction until everything is settled.

The following suggestions may seem unimportant, but it is advised for the official closing. You should have the following documents made available:

Present the homeowners' insurance policy, this will prove you have protection for your property.

Have your checkbook available to pay for the closing costs.

Present your mortgage check from the lender.

Receive the warranty deed with the signature of the seller.

Your attorney should record legal documents with the local county courthouse and check for any liens.

Your new keys to your home will be given to you.

Now you are ready to sign the closing paperwork, read each page carefully, including the fine print, because this will create a major impact on your finances and your life for years to come. Verify that your interest rate is correct and there is no "prepayment penalty." Compare your closing costs to the good faith estimate you had been presented with at the beginning of the process. If any fees are off by 10 percent, *by all means question this.*

Final Walk-Through

After the process of purchasing your home is completed, it is recommended to do a final walk-through. The will give you the opportunity and last chance to make sure that everything is in working order. If it is not, there is still time to raise any issues, this may avoid costly repairs down the road or if you decide, you can have the time to back out of the deal. Make yourself a checklist including the following:

Working appliances: Upon walking in the door, turn on the dishwasher, the oven and flush the toilets to make sure there are no leaks. Does anything seem out of the ordinary, ask and make sure you are satisfied with the response.

> Working plumbing: Turn every faucet and shower head and then turn them off. Are there any drips? How is the water pressure? Check pipes underneath the sink and basement, if this is a private home to see any apparent leaks.
>
> Major systems: Turn on the central heat and air. Are they working, stay around long enough feel if the temperature has changed and not just hearing the systems blowing.
>
> Remotes and keypads: If this is a private home and has a home security system does the keypad work? If any of the rooms have remote control fans, do they work?
>
> Landscaping: Check the grounds of your home, some people take plants with them. Check to see if there is an irrigation system and make sure it works too.
>
> Lights and other fixtures: Make sure all lights and switch plates are in place.

Repairs: The sellers may have had been required to make certain repairs or upgrades before they move out. Make sure that any projects are completed. Bring an issue up if you should find something was not completed.

Cleanliness: The seller is required to leave the home clean and free of their possessions. Make sure all appliances, i.e., refrigerator is absolutely clean and emptied. The garage and yard are emptied and clean.

We were amazed after we purchased our condominium that the seller had really cleaned and left us some valuable things as patio chairs, cleaning materials, garden boxes for the patio, a great vacuum cleaner, and a large painting. We thought this was such a generous gesture.

Credits

Book:

The *Wall Street Journal. Complete Home Owner's Guidebook*: *Make the Most of Your Biggest Asset in any Market*. David Crook. 2008. New York: Dow Jones. Inc/Three River Press, Crown Publishing Group of Random House, Inc.

About the Author

Judith D. Dickson, is the sole author of this book, *A Successful and Proven Guide for the First Time Homebuyer: Putting It All Together*. Based upon firsthand experience purchasing a home, she gives a detailed guide that covers everything a first time buyer would want to know from hiring a real estate agent to the closing on the home.

Judith is a member of Cambridge Who's Who, National Association of Independent Writers, and Professional Writers Alliance. She has written articles for Women of Distinction Magazine, Executive Business Alliance, and National Women's Book Association, Boston Chapter. She completed writing courses at Gotham Writers' Workshop, New York, and the Writers' Digest University, the School of Visual Arts, New York, and American Bar Association. Judith holds a bachelor's degree in fine arts from Boston University and is attending the University of Southern New Hampshire for her master's degree in English and Creative Writing. Before she began writing as her second career, she had worked within private industry. Her passion for writing has made her life more significant. Judith's favorite publications are the *New York Times*, *Writer's Digest*, *Writers and Poets Magazines*, *The New Yorker Magazine*, and *Writers Weekly*. Judith and her significant other, Robert, reside in Connecticut.

www.ingramcontent.com/pod-product-compliance
Lightning Source LLC
Chambersburg PA
CBHW031506210526
45463CB00003B/1110